Praise for *Walking the Refuge* by Glenn Watt

"It's said that birds in renaissance paintings represent transcendence—whether for their gift of hypnotic song or ability to skip so easily along the trusses of heaven. Regardless, birds have inspired great artists and writers throughout the centuries. Glenn Watt's *Walking the Refuge* is one such inspired and welcomed work. Through his keen eye and exquisitely musical line, Watt creates not just a fine homage to the mysterious life of birds, but offers a deeper commentary on the nourishing power of time spent alone in nature, an increasingly rare luxury these days. Reading Watt's poems I'm reminded of both Gary Snyder's rich descriptions of the American West and Wendell Berry's quiet reverence for the pastures of Kentucky—which also include, like the poems in *Walking the Refuge*, the subliminal questions of purpose and stewardship. In these poems, Watt captures so clearly the personality of birds, their innocence and simplicity, as well as their brilliance and comedy. It's easy to imagine Watt out wading alone in the prairie grasses of the Midwest, at sunrise or sunset, when the communities of birds are most vigorous (or the distractions of humanity least), with binoculars or naked eye, completely absorbed in the sensations, subtleties and nuances of pure nature. Here is his poem "Fledgling," in its entirety, which exemplifies so much of what these poems achieve:

Can we say the immature and still flightless
kestrel, venturing to the edge
of its portal into this world
in a plastered church bell tower —
we humans tending our graves below,
the neighborhood chatter of work and play —
does not nor ever will have a past
or a future, what we might call memory,
but rather a gradual layering up
of impressions over time, a buoyancy
in the bones for flight, iridescent scrabble
of vole urine trails in the grass,
giving rise to a familiarity, a kind of affection
for what is: blood, flesh, the stiff salt breeze
off the fjord, the ringing of the bell?"

—Christopher Seid, Author of *Age of Exploration*
and *Prayers To the Other Life*

"These poems, like their subjects, dart about, surprise, reveal, hide... Watt is a devotee of the world, his ear and eye fastened to the ground. His diligent naming of what is seen approaches a kind of prayer: the sounds seed-like versions of the birds themselves. The music in these poems is well-earned; you can hear, in between its sudden, delightful eruptions, the waiting and watching, the long silences."

—Mermer Blakeslee, Author of *When You Live by a River*
and *A Conversation with Fear*

"This poet says, "Each spring, unknown to most of us,/ our lives are flooded by the lives of others..." How lucky we are to have this alert guide, whose eyes are wide open to the flood of pulsating life. He makes us realize how much this earth is our home, the only one we have, and that we are it, the earth, the stars, the endless. What kind of miracle are you going to encounter today? This poet says, "Sometimes we get to meet one/ all by itself/ stripped down and vital/and hardly a handspan tall/ worrying the last vestige of spring wetness/ along the weedy edge/ of a still fallow farm field/ doing whatever it can/ like the rest of us/ to fatten itself up/ for the unknown/ the inevitable next leg of the journey." Long may we travel with such a companion."

—Rustin Larson, Author of *The Philosopher Savant*
(Glass Lyre Press, 2015)

"At this time when so many of us are tethered to technology, fixated on a small screen even while walking in this world, Glenn Watt's poems call to us like birdsong to look up, listen and reconnect to the living earth. These poems provide a "refuge" for the reader, echoing the visionary tradition in American letters of Henry David Thoreau and A.R. Ammons, who knew the best way to liberate and enrich the Self is in the natural world."

—Steven P. Schneider, Author of *A.R. Ammons and the Poetics of Widening Scope*
and editor of *The Contemporary Narrative Poem: Critical Crosscurrents.*

WALKING THE REFUGE

Glenn Watt

BLUE LIGHT PRESS ◆ 1ST WORLD PUBLISHING

1ST WORLD
PUBLISHING

SAN FRANCISCO ◆ FAIRFIELD ◆ DELHI

WINNER OF THE 2015 BLUE LIGHT POETRY PRIZE
WALKING THE REFUGE

Copyright ©2016 by Glenn Watt

1ST WORLD LIBRARY
PO Box 2211
Fairfield, IA 52556
www.1stworldpublishing.com

BLUE LIGHT PRESS
www.bluelightpress.com
Email: bluelightpress@aol.com

BOOK & COVER DESIGN
Melanie Gendron
www.melaniegendron.com

COVER ART
"Red Tail Red Butte" by Sally Watt

FIRST EDITION

ISBN 978-1-4218-3752-9

"Birds make me happier
than stop signs."

—my daughter Sessily, age 4

Contents

Sunday Morning

Sunday morning
end of a three day soaker
misting but with the promise of a reprieve

the remnants of Ike scraping
across the southeast corner of the state
Cedar over its banks at the bridge
Ely and Duckworth scoured,
still boot high and running fast.

What a sweet place this planet can be
sometimes —

Catbirds like pieces of charcoal in the wet leaves,
mossy backs of the Chestnuts.

At least down here, right now —

persistent ratchet of a nervous Black-billed
like someone cinching down a bolt,
Swainsons' mobbing the dogwood,
moonseed and wild grape.

Plenty in this world to get agitated over,
plenty to be thankful for,
the mind and its juggernaut flights —

like these acrobatic Least, solo Yellow-bellied
pinching flies out of thin air —

its fits of twists and tumbles and spins
high bar to high bar,

the trick to learn how to land
back on your feet, ready for anything.

In this case, the next wave of neotropics
like a sudden flush of endorphins
racing through the dendritic bushes and trees —

fleeting, effervescent, unpredictable,
at the moment, all there is.

Exactly Nothing

Skipping work
I haul my guilt
through the fog
and pre-dawn dark
to the mecca
of prairie cordgrass
along the russet banks
of Buckshot pond
and arrive
just as the sun
begins to break
over my shoulders
and onto the golden
chest high grasses
and gather about me
my implements of worship
and wade out
into this sea of glory
to pay homage
to one of these rare
and perky migrants
of this planet
who tell me
exactly nothing
which is exactly
what I have come
to hear.

Fledgling

Can we say the immature and still flightless
kestrel, venturing to the edge
of its portal into this world
in a plastered church bell tower —
we humans tending our graves below,
the neighborhood chatter of work and play —
does not nor ever will have a past
or a future, what we might call memory,
but rather a gradual layering up
of impressions over time, a buoyancy
in the bones for flight, iridescent scrabble
of vole urine trails in the grass,
giving rise to a familiarity, a kind of affection
for what is: blood, flesh, the stiff salt breeze
off the fjord, the ringing of the bell?

—after Mikael Kristersson's documentary *Kestrel's Eye*

Keeping Score

Why not something simple
at the start, like this variegated
flake or scale of bark
sidling up and around
the pale trunks of sound
before busting out the chops,
the bops and bobs
of eighths and sixteenths tossed
at random across the stubbed
rhythms, the chiseled riffs
all stacked and stitched with these
twitchy short-tailed tones
teased out of the tune
to flit and dart, bunched up
and fleeting about the edges,
among the windbent, overgrown stems.

"...the myriad petals..."

Then each pilfered glimpse
of this short eared owl prowling
the unshorn, snow-flattened fields before us
at dusk —

soft hinge of its body unfurled,
wings like long leaves flared and fluttering,
twin barrels for eyes,
breastplate of finely hammered gold

flashing against the bloody
mauves and violets, molten oranges
and icy turquoise-blues,

against a backlit indigo screen of trees —

each relentless, moth-like, appetite-driven
dip and sweep

a petal off that flower
dissolving even as it opens and falls.

—after a line by Peter Matthiessen from *End of the World*

The Truth

The truth, this morning, fidgets and preens
on a slightly elevated wire before me.

It has a long bill that it shoves joyfully
down the throat of beauty.

It has a curious eye
and large, green scales that shimmer in the sun.

There is not a single concept inside its head.

It is so small and quick, I think
nothing can feed on it.

Though look at me, ravenous
as the rest.

Sundown at Otter Creek

As if a ghost
of its former glamorous self
in its late season grays and whites,

the much simpler splendor
of a single slender-necked
fall Phalarope feeding

chest deep at dusk
in the lapping platinum shallows,

performing its own little dinnertime
version of a cha cha
for the neighborhood waders and peeps,

the big red lazy ball of the sun
sinking slowly behind it
as a backdrop

and all around,
large billowing sheets of blackbirds
ripped from the clothesline of summer

and sent racing, like time itself,
over the tops of the trees.

On The Sheetwater

Here
on the sheetwater
in a script
I could never
imagine
fourteen black
and white bodies
bending
over the bright
blue pencils
of legs
long orange necks
and heads down
sweeping side to side
in the shallows
in the muck
in the shimmering
blankness
of the unknown
as if feeding
on the invisible
itself
as they march
voracious
as they prowl
in a compact
column
back and forth
between the thin
broken
and barely discernible
shoals

a song
without a singer
days and days later
still singing
inside me.

Nelson's Sharp-Tail

Who wouldn't want to replicate it? Who wouldn't
want to make it again and again new?

In the raw wind, beneath a bruised sky,
it stepped up onto the world's stage
and I kid you not, the clouds cracked open like curtains
and the sun, whom we hadn't seen all day,
broke through.

We think of them as drab, call them
"little brown jobs", but no —

ocheraceous, the book says, and for the juvenile,
more ocheraceous.

As if someone, you know who, took a healthy pinch
of that orange-yellow powder,
mixed it with the word outrageous,
and tossed it into the willows.

And then, as all things of beauty do, it fled.

—after Elaine Scarry's *On Beauty and Being Just*

Bubo Virginianus Virginianus

Like witnessing the soul

flushed out of a half-frozen,
dead birch and maple stippled marsh,

and holding up, small miracle,
at the tail end of a sparse run
of still-living trees —

glimpse of ear tufts, feathered belly,
large preternatural eye through limb clutter
at a hundred yards —

then gone
when you try to make your move.

Common Yellowthroat

I was all ready to dismiss it
in its chartreuse shirt and oversized black mask
as just another one of those —

even the name we've given it
is a kind of pejorative,
as in the common housefly or the common cold —

but then, reed stalk to reed stalk,
it sauntered over
through the trees of its country estate,

which this roadside ditch probably was,
as if to lean on the car door
and say hello.

Not hello exactly,
but with that same gesture
of curiosity and common courtesy,

and not all the way to the door
either, but if it had,
what could I have said,

bellied up to the window
with this bird
we might, at one moment, exalt in song,

and the next, spray
in its ditch of weeds?

Timber Doodle

We too have stood at the edge
in the fading light, waiting
for Mr. Big-Eyes, the bogsucker,
that spends its days hiding,
its nights face down in the mud,
long articulate bill sniffing out
the chemical trails of earthworms,
ears shoved forward of the eyes
to hear them, eyes shoved
to the top of the head to see us,
upside down brain to accommodate both,
in a flurry of stubby wings,
haul its plump, pear-shaped body
and strange, insect-like call
out into a clearing to strut and peeent
until it is driven, *out of lust*
and seemingly against its very nature,
upward, a dark speck two hundred feet
above us, circling against the stars,
then the long-arced spiral of descent,
wind chirping through slots in its wings,
canary-like twittering, the final, wild,
leaf-like tumble back to earth
where the females wait and the peenting
begins again and again, *out of lust,*
let's say, for this sudden life.

From Our Vantage Here On The Ground

Like a scrap of code —
protean, ribonucleic, neuropeptidal —

a scrim, a fragment
of some larger communication,

some vast organic process invisible
from our vantage here on the ground,

a lone undulating rhythmic string
winging and singing itself

purposefully through the thin blue
liquid envelope overhead,

hauling its age-old message, its memory,
all its accumulated joys and sorrows

north over the lip of the world.

Miracles

Sometimes we get to meet one
all by itself

stripped down and vital
and hardly a handspan tall

worrying the last vestige of spring wetness
along the weedy edge
of a still fallow farm field

doing whatever it can
like the rest of us
to fatten itself up

for the unknown
the inevitable next leg of the journey.

Sometimes we get to meet one
up close
as if it's no big deal

just a couple of strangers
going about their brief business on this planet
momentarily shoulder to shoulder
in the weeds.

Now That The Migration Is Over

As if we were standing around together
out on the lawn at a potluck
during the rapture

when all the gaily colored and oddly shaped souls,
finally released from their earthly prison,
came whizzing by

in one long ragged magnificent tittering flock,

leaving the rest of us momentarily stunned,
swirling like bits of leaves and dust
in the aftermath of some great passing.

Mourning

He is standing, like a fickle god,
looking down —

a dozen feet below him,
adrift in the luxuriant green
undergrowth of spring,

a bird he could easily tuck
into the protective cup of a single palm
is plying the riprap of decaying
logs and limbs for bugs,

its dark indigo hood draped
like a funereal shroud
down around its yellow breast,

the splotches about its eyes
like mascara permanently smeared
into tears

as if it has spent its whole life traveling
from one tragedy to another,

though the bird appears anything but sad
as it feeds intently on spiders, beetles and grubs
plucked like fruit
from the surrounding tangle

during this brief stay
in its long arduous journey north.

Through what difficulty did it just come?
he wonders, leaning against the rail,
toward what difficulty must it soon go?

his attention already turning, caught
like a cat by the next
peripatetic quiver in the leaves.

Here Comes One Now

It must be mostly a guy thing
to get up, but not too early,
slip into your finest
and motor to the next big town over
where all the pretty gulls gather
to hang, mingle and promenade,
mewling and squawking,
along the river, this time to zoom in
on an errant California gem
dressed like a tramp
in pink lipstick and stockings,
and there she is now, swooping
in and out among the locals,
everybody caught up in the excitement,
wheeling around for another run
down the gauntlet, or peeling off
to idle, primp and preen
in twos and threes among the milling
throngs, the bystanders and onlookers,
all of us in our various ways
here to feed on the dazed
windfall of this — the only joint
open for miles.

Busting the Loop

It's the annual spring mixer
at Cone —

mid-March, sunny but crisp,
wind down, water mostly iced over,
thin sheets of cirrus mares-tailing overhead —

and we're busting the long loop,
winter-snarled snag, boot-suck,
toe-trip, log-woven bog

off trail to skirt any unnecessary
disruption in the gabbling masses,
raft after raft of them,
primped and pumped to mate,

long sensuous lines of the slender-necked
cracker, metallic green sheen
of the duck-tailed frenchy, moon bill,
black jack, swaddle-bill broady,
fat white forehead stripe of the campy
whistler, speckle-belly, bull-neck,
red-headed broadbill, green-winged mud hen,
lone bride working the congested
slots along the back,

even the black-headed honker,
yellow-legged laugher, blue-winged
wavey, barking snow
beyond the narrow northern dike,

the din of them, the bluster,
clamor of shrill plaintive bleets, mewlings,
smacks and whistles,

constant criss-cross of fly-bys —

if we can't, as the wise say,
speak the truth,
we can still show up,
wrinkle-faced wobbly, purple-bellied gawker,
and revel in its display.

When The Urge Is Upon Us

Is it any wonder when the urge is upon us
and we are no bigger than a small child's hand
and weigh not much more than a small child's
handful of tissues and yet we fly
ambitiously and with fervid splendor
two, three, sometimes five thousand miles,
braving torrential head and sheer and cross
winds of hurricanes and tropical storms,
cold fronts, lightning and hail, a rare
late snow or freezing rain, rarer tornado,
braving communication towers and their guy wires,
wind farms, tall buildings, even light houses
lost in low lying cloud cover in the dark,
braving horrors of predation, braving
constant gut-wrenching hunger
from the outer edges and humps and hollows
of the tail end of the undulating bony spine
of our beginning out across the great
unmoored and unmooring gulf
and up the long, fertile, meandering crease
with its many branching tributaries
to arrive once again, exhausted and joyful,
on our rich, abundant breeding grounds and mate
and mate when the urge is upon us?

Polyglot

Down at
        kohw kohw kohw kohw kohw kohw
Croton in the early morning chill,
a wood wraith, an operatic
                toop toop toop
spook stages up each spring
in an overgrown creek bottom amphitheater at
                                ee ee

forest's edge, a dense thicket
of throaty, multi-syllabic
                kaw kaw
call-notes punctuating the hollow,
a polyglot cacophony of
                    urururururururur
words and song, as if when the body
collapses, what moves on
                    mraaAa mraaAa
is a voice, and one of them,
body-less, not quite ready to go, is spilling back
                                  chkchkchkchk
over from that other world
to haunt for a little while longer
                    yit yit yit

this one.

The Gleaning

As if the tree had birthed them
out of some singular willed desire
for flight, they appeared
in the mid-morning calm suddenly
at the oak's rain-soaked tips
and, fruit of its fruit, pinched free
in twos and threes and fours at first
to dart across the creekbed's gash
of sky, fifty, sixty in all
streaming like spindrift off its crest
to skitter and jig, ravenous,
branch to branch, bay-breasted
and blackpoll, blackburnian and pine,
parula, nashville, tennessee,
gold-winged, redstart, chestnut-sided,
black-and-white, wilson's, canada,
black-throated green winging it
by, a rogue wave, a frenzied gleaning
loosed upon the world to wheel
and buck and veer overhead,
all sputter and surge, all cut and run
through the leaf-heavy limbs
to abruptly balk and stall, circle
and settle like late-morning rain
more leisurely down to feed
and finally, by noon, leaf to leaf,
layer upon layer, fade
slowly back into the trees,
the surrounding wood scoured clean.

Warbler-Necking At Lacey

May 3, 2002

Each spring, unknown to most of us,
our lives are flooded by the lives of others,

> *flaring rump patch of a Myrtle*
> *sallying for flies in the oaks*
>
> *that little skulker, the Common Yellowthroat, skulking*
> *the multiflora at forest's edge*
>
> *teacher! teacher! teacher! of an elusive Ovenbird*
> *deeper in*

storm-tossed, insect and bud dependent,
they come.

> *white spectacle of a Blue-Headed Vireo*
>
> *canary-yellow Blue-Winged's thin black mask*

They raid the lush, gladed creek bottoms,

> *flitty Nashville, its white eye ring, its sooty hood*
>
> *faint streaked breast of an Orange-Crowned*
>
> *tail-pumping Palm passing through*

the log-toppled ravines, the copses
and brushy edges,

Yellow-Throated finally — early arriver, early leaver —
nesting in Sycamore by the bridge

dark auburn necklace of a Northern Parula

wade bare-legged through knee-high poison ivy,
snuggle into gooseberry and rose,

clown-faced Kentucky — right in front of us! —
casting its voice farther out

flit through the fingertips of trees.

quick glimpse of a Blackpoll skylined
in walnut tips — a first for us both

And no matter how much we plan, study, calculate,

lazy drawl of a Yellow-Throated Vireo
picking casually past

they always show up by grace, and by grace alone,

warbling of a Warbling Vireo out the car window

black bead eye, big black beak of a Prothonotary
low in just leafing honeysuckle along the bank

appear and disappear
as if out of some invisible magician's hat,

Louisiana Waterthrush butt-bob by the dam

layered-up sour-noted background-chat
of a Red-Eyed Vireo

because it is, and always will be, their show all along.

red and black Redstart tail flash
deep in dogwood

brilliant chestnut cheek patch,
bold black-lined breast of a spring Cape May.

Prayer

May we too
pass through this brief
and sudden beauty
that is our lives
as simply and joyfully
as the kinglet
when it flings itself
and its tiny beating heart
wide eyed
and without reservation
through the tangle
of interlacing limbs
and blossoms
that at this moment
is the fleeting portal
of its own.

About the Author

Originally from Wyoming, Glenn has spent the last three decades walking and birding the Chariton, Des Moines, and Iowa river ecosystems of southeastern Iowa. Except for "Fledgling", which came from a film, all of these poems had their origins here. Many thanks to the birds and to those of us who have strived to maintain their habitats.